561,5982

S0-AGA-006

Ecosystems Research Journal

Galapagos Islands Research Journal

Natalie Hyde

CRABTREE
PUBLISHING COMPANY
WWW.CRABTREEBOOKS.COM

CRABTREE
PUBLISHING COMPANY
WWW.CRABTREEBOOKS.COM

Author: Natalie Hyde

Editors: Sonya Newland, Kathy Middleton

Design: Clare Nicholas

Cover design: Abigail Smith

Proofreader: Wendy Scavuzzo

**Production coordinator and
prepress technician:** Tammy McGarr

Print coordinator: Katherine Berti

Produced for Crabtree Publishing Company
by White-Thomson Publishing

Library and Archives Canada Cataloguing in Publication

Hyde, Natalie, 1963-, author
      Galapagos Islands research journal / Natalie Hyde.

(Ecosystems research journal)
Includes index.
Issued in print and electronic formats.
ISBN 978-0-7787-4661-4 (hardcover).--
ISBN 978-0-7787-4674-4 (softcover).--
ISBN 978-1-4271-2065-6 (HTML)

      1. Biotic communities--Galapagos Islands--Juvenile literature.
2. Island ecology--Galapagos Islands--Juvenile literature.
3. Ecology--Galapagos Islands--Juvenile literature. I. Title.

QH198.G3H93 2018   j577.5'2098665   C2017-907623-X
                                          C2017-907624-8

Library of Congress Cataloging-in-Publication Data

CIP Available at the Library of Congress

Crabtree Publishing Company

www.crabtreebooks.com   1-800-387-7650

Printed in the U.S.A./022018/CG20171220

Published in Canada
Crabtree Publishing
616 Welland Ave.
St. Catharines, Ontario
L2M 5V6

Published in the United States
Crabtree Publishing
PMB 59051
350 Fifth Avenue, 59th Floor
New York, New York 10118

Published in the United Kingdom
Crabtree Publishing
Maritime House
Basin Road North, Hove
BN41 1WR

Published in Australia
Crabtree Publishing
3 Charles Street
Coburg North
VIC, 3058

Contents

Mission to the Galapagos Islands

Bartolomé Island in the Galapagos

As a **biologist**, I study animals all over the world. Today, I got an invitation to observe some of the most unusual animals on the planet! The Volcanic Research Organization asked me to report on the Galapagos Islands. Biologist Charles Darwin visited the Galapagos in 1835. He studied the wildlife on the islands. These studies helped him form his theory of how plants and animals **adapt**, or change, to suit their environments. There are plants and animals on these volcanic islands that do not exist anywhere else on Earth.

4

Darwin Island

Wolf Island

Ecuador volcano
Wolf volcano
Punta Vicente Roca
Santiago Island
Pacific Ocean
Bartolemé Island
Urbina Bay
Isabela Island
Santa Cruz Island
Fernandina Island
Elizabeth Bay
San Cristóbal Island
Sierra Negra volcano
Santa Fé Island
Puerto Villamil
Las Tintoreras
The Tunnels

The Galapagos Islands are part of Ecuador and lie about 600 miles (970 kilometers) off the country's coast. They were formed by volcanoes. There are 13 larger islands and 6 smaller ones, as well as many tiny islands. In 1978, the United Nations made the islands a World Heritage Site. Now, 97 percent of the land and water around the islands are protected areas. Humans are allowed to live on 3 percent of the land. More than 25,000 people live in this small area. This helps protect the rare and unusual wildlife living there. For hundreds of years, there were no people nearby that could affect or change the plants or wildlife. But today, the habitat is under threat. Eruptions, earthquakes, tourism, and human activities are changing the **ecosystem**.

I am looking forward to seeing some unique animals and birds on the islands, such as the magnificent frigate bird.

Darwin noticed how plants and animals had adapted to life on the Galapagos islands here. For example, the beak of a species of bird might change over time to suit the kind of food available to eat on an island. He thought such changes helped the plant or animal to survive and reproduce there. He called this theory **evolution**.

5

Field Journal: Day 1

Fernandina Island

I talked with a **volcanologist** this morning. She is working on Fernandina Island, watching the volcanic activity in the Galapagos. The islands that are farther west are still forming and changing. They have active volcanoes. The volcanoes that created the islands in the eastern part of the chain are no longer active. They haven't erupted in more than one million years. Fernandina is the youngest island of the chain. Its volcano still erupts. The latest eruption was in 2009.

There is life even in the lava fields on Fernandina Island.

6

Even though much of Fernandina is covered in jet-black rock made of hardened **lava**, plants and animals still live here. The island is home to rice rats, lava lizards, and the lava cactus. Sally Lightfoot crabs live on the shore. Marine iguanas, sea lions, and the Galapagos hawk hunt and fish in the shallow water around the island. There is only one site on the island where tourists are allowed. This helps keep the impact humans have on the wildlife low.

Sally Lightfoot crab

Sea lions and marine iguanas live side by side on Fernandina Island.

natstat **STATUS** REPORT ST456/part B

Name: Brown sea cucumber
(Isostichopus fuscus)

Threats:
Overfishing, **climate change**

Description:
Sea cucumbers have long, tube-like bodies. Brown sea cucumbers in the Galapagos live in shallow water. They feed on bits of algae or tiny animals. The food they break down becomes food for bacteria. Their eggs and young are **prey** for fish and other marine animals. Sea cucumbers are fished to sell in markets in Asia. There they are considered a tasty treat. Low numbers due to overfishing have forced Ecuador to close the fishery in the Galapagos.

Status:
Endangered, and numbers are still going down

Attach photograph here →

7

Field Journal: Day 2

Puerto Villamil, Isabela Island

Isabela is the largest of the Galapagos Islands. It also has active volcanoes, including Wolf volcano, which erupted in 2015. Only four Galapagos Islands have people living on them. They are mostly farmers and fishermen. Many people live in the port town of Villamil on Isabela Island. The sidewalks are made with lava **pavers**. There is only one traffic stop—the Iguana Crossing. It allows a safe route for iguanas between the beach and **lagoons**. Even police stop to let the animals pass! It shows how people living there care about their environment.

Puerto Villamil has a population of around 2,200.

Marine iguana

Sightings

The cormorant has lost its ability to fly. It had no predators on the island to flee from and nowhere to fly to.

Flightless cormorant

8

Outside the town is a breeding center for giant tortoises. The Galapagos giant tortoise was close to extinction. Sailors and settlers had hunted them for food. Goats and pigs brought by whalers competed with the tortoises for food. The breeding center has helped change the giant tortoise's decreasing numbers. Researchers began to remove the goats and pigs, and the tortoises began to thrive again. The center also helps raise young tortoises. Once they are old enough, they are released into the wild.

↑ Young giant tortoises at the breeding center

natstat STATUS REPORT ST456/part B

Name: Sierra Negra giant tortoise (Chelonoidis nigra guentheri)

Description:

This tortoise lives on the southern slopes of the Sierra Negra volcano. Its shell is flat on top, like a table. It grazes for most of the day. It eats cactus fruit, grass, leaves, melons, and oranges. It gets water from dew and from its food. This tortoise can go without drinking for more than six months. It lays its eggs on dry, sandy beaches. Young hatch after four to eight months.

Attach photograph here ➡

Threats:
Hunting for food, habitat loss, competition for food from other animals

Numbers:
About 700

Status:
Endangered

Field Journal: Day 3

Snorkeling at The Tunnels, Isabela Island

Today, I went **snorkeling** at a place called The Tunnels, off the south coast of Isabela. Lava flowing underground created caves and tunnels here. Many birds and marine animals make The Tunnels their home. I saw albatrosses and blue-footed boobies on the banks. Penguins, manta rays, and sea snakes feed among the rock formations. The landscape is always changing. Strong waves cause the lava rock to weaken and **erode**. Arches and tubes collapse, and eruptions form new structures.

Blue-footed booby

Blue-footed boobies live on the rocks of Las Tintoreras. These birds can be identified by their bright-blue feet. Each bird's feet are a different shade of blue. Scientists believe the brighter blue a bird's feet are, the healthier the bird is.

At The Tunnels, lava has also cooled above ground to form arches.

10

In the afternoon, I took a dinghy to Las Tintoreras. This is a chain of islets (tiny islands) off the coast near Villamil. The bay is clear and shallow. Coral growing here provides food and shelter for fish. Warmer water from climate change is harming, and even killing, the coral colonies. The bay is connected to the sea by a **crevice** made of lava rock. It is filled with water when the **tide** is high. Whitetip sharks like to **bask** in the sun here. There are also colonies of Galapagos sea lions here.

Las Tintoreras

natstat STATUS REPORT ST456/part B

Name: *Whitetip reef shark (Triaenodon obesus)*

Threats:
Habitat destruction

Description:

These sharks are known by the white tip on their dorsal, or top, fin. They like the shallow water around coral. Whitetips are very social animals. Large groups often rest together. They hunt at night. Their favorite foods are eels, octopuses, lobsters, and crabs. Fishermen do not catch whitetip sharks because their meat is **toxic** to humans.

Numbers:
Unknown

Status:
Near threatened

Attach photograph here

11

Field Journal: Day 4

Sierra Negra and Wolf Craters

I wanted to explore the plants and animals that live on the **craters** of the volcanoes that formed the Galapagos Islands. First I headed to Sierra Negra, which is a shield volcano. Shield volcanoes are shaped like domes. Each time they erupt, the fast-flowing lava covers large areas. As the lava slows, it cools. It creates new rock and new landscapes. The island constantly changes and grows larger. At the base of the volcano, I saw lots of trees and wildlife. Up near the rim, I noticed that the ground is dry. The only moisture it gets is brought by clouds. Along the path near the rim, I saw a flowering guava tree, but this tree doesn't grow fruit.

Sightings

I spotted a Galapagos hawk on its nest on a lava ledge. If the nest is disturbed by humans, the parents will abandon it.

Galapagos hawk

The crater of the Sierra Negra volcano

12

Wolf volcano had not erupted for 33 years before the 2015 eruption.

Pink iguana

Later, I headed over to the crater of Wolf volcano. This is the home of critically endangered rosy iguanas. I was worried because I knew Wolf had erupted in 2015. I wasn't sure that any pink iguanas survived. I joined with scientists to check on them. We climbed the northern side of the crater. Several iguanas were sunning themselves on rocks. Luckily, they survived the eruption. The iguanas are also prey for animals that are not native to Isabela. Black rats and **feral** cats accidentally brought by sailing ships hunt iguanas. **Conservation** projects are working to rid the islands of these **invasive species**. Scientists may also try to breed the iguanas in zoos.

1813   1817   1844
1860   1911   1948   1953
1954   1957   1963
1979   2005

Years When Sierra Negra Has Erupted

13

Field Journal: Day 5

Elizabeth Bay and the Mariela Islets

Old lava flows have created shallow lagoons around the islands. This is an important habitat for many animals that live in the sea. Elizabeth Bay and the Mariela Islets lie off the western coast of Isabela. The bay is a resting and feeding place for all kinds of wildlife, such as sea turtles. I decided to take a kayak out to have a closer look. To protect the wildlife there, no visitors are allowed on these tiny islands. The largest marine iguanas live here. They feed on the algae.

Sightings

I managed to identify a lava heron, cleverly camouflaged. Its gray color allows it to blend in with the hardened lava.

Lava heron

Elizabeth Bay

14

Around the edges of Elizabeth Bay are red and black mangroves. The roots of black mangroves stick out of the water. This is so the **bristles** can take in more oxygen. Red mangroves grow **prop roots**, which carry air to the roots underwater. They are covered with a kind of wax to keep the salt out. Mangroves are an important ecosystem. Their roots are a nursery for young animals, providing them with food and protection as they grow. The roots also cling to the soil, helping to prevent shore erosion.

Mangroves are trees that live in shallow, salty water. ↓

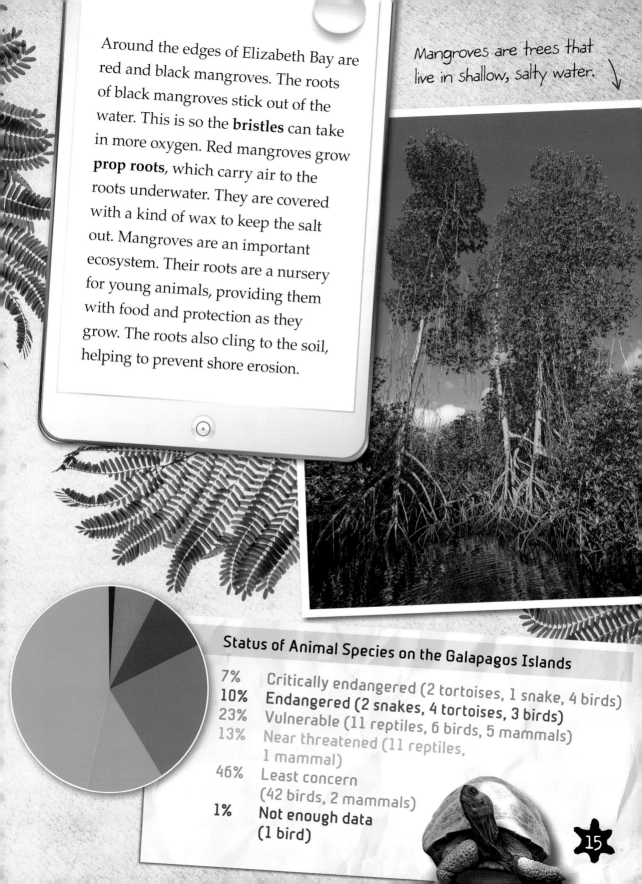

Status of Animal Species on the Galapagos Islands

7%	Critically endangered (2 tortoises, 1 snake, 4 birds)
10%	Endangered (2 snakes, 4 tortoises, 3 birds)
23%	Vulnerable (11 reptiles, 6 birds, 5 mammals)
13%	Near threatened (11 reptiles, 1 mammal)
46%	Least concern (42 birds, 2 mammals)
1%	Not enough data (1 bird)

15

Field Journal: Day 6

I listened to the sounds of the Nazca boobies: the female squawks while the male whistles.

Punta Vicente Roca

I stayed on the west side of Isabela Island today to snorkel at Punta Vicente Roca. This marine-only visitor site is along a rock wall formed by the Ecuador volcano. Ecuador is the only volcano in the Galapagos that has not erupted in the recorded history of the islands. But the rock formations that still exist from old eruptions are amazing. I took a small boat to the dive site. The wall was part of the volcano crater. It is home to many animals. I saw seahorses, parrot fish, and frog fish. I turned around to see a Port Jackson shark. This bullhead shark is rare but harmless.

Back aboard the boat, I sailed close to some vertical rocks. They are part of the old crater. The Cromwell Current is a deep ocean current that flows east. It carries oxygen and a food supply to this area. I could see that the extra food brought many animals and birds together. At one point, I saw a feeding frenzy. Dolphins, sea lions, pelicans, and great blue herons were feeding on the many fish brought by the current. The frenzy was interrupted by more boats arriving to watch. Tourism is growing quickly in the Galapagos.

↑ More than 150,000 tourists visit the Galapagos each year. The more tourists that come to the Galapagos Islands, the bigger the impact on wildlife.

natstat STATUS REPORT ST456/part B

Name: Sunfish (Mola mola)

Description:

Also known as the common mola, this is a flat, bony sunfish. It swims on its side to soak up more sunlight. It eats mainly jellyfish. It has to eat a lot of them to get enough nutrition. Females produce 300 million eggs at a time. These fish are hunted by tuna, sea lions, orca, and sharks.

Attach photograph here ➡

Threats:
Caught in nets and fishing lines set to catch other kinds of fish

Numbers:
18,000

Status:
Vulnerable, and numbers are decreasing

17

Wolf Island →

Diving at Northern Wolf and Darwin Islands

I sailed north of the main Galapagos Islands this morning. I'm planning to go scuba diving near some of the smallest islands. Darwin and Wolf islands are the remains of extinct volcanoes. They are some distance away from the rest of the islands. That makes them vulnerable to illegal fishing. The Galapagos National Park has established a floating base at Wolf Island. It is used to patrol the area and protect wildlife.

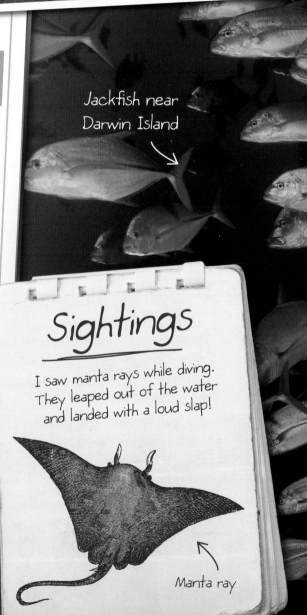

Jackfish near Darwin Island

Sightings

I saw manta rays while diving. They leaped out of the water and landed with a loud slap!

Manta ray

18

I am going to stay on a liveaboard—a floating home for divers. We are allowed to explore the water around the islands, but we cannot go on land. Near Darwin Island, I saw a rock arch called Darwin's Arch. Diving down, I felt strong currents and cold water. This area is only for experienced divers. As I explored underwater, I came face to face with a huge group of hammerhead sharks and whale sharks. There were also schools of jack fish and eagle rays. Back onboard, I used binoculars to view Darwin Island. It is the only nesting place for a bird called the sooty tern.

Scalloped hammerhead sharks are common in the waters around the Galapagos Islands.

natstat STATUS REPORT ST456/part B

Name: Vampire ground finch (*Geospiza septentrionalis*)

Threats:
Limited habitat, invasive species, bird flu

Description:
The male and female of this finch are different colors. Males are black. Females are gray with brown streaks. Vampire ground finches drink the blood of other birds. They peck the skin of Nazca and blue-footed boobies until they break it. Surprisingly, the boobies do not seem to react to this. The finches also eat bird eggs. They roll them out of nests until they fall and break open on the rocks.

Numbers:
250–999 adults

Status:
Vulnerable

Attach photograph here ➡

19

Field Journal: Day 8

Santiago Island

Salted fish

Santiago Island

Heading south again, I am off to Santiago Island. This used to be a landing spot for whalers and sailors. They would stop here for water, wood, and food. Spanish sailors also mined salt here. They used salt to preserve their fish and tortoise meat for long voyages. The salt mine they built was used until 1960. Now it is a tourist attraction. When Charles Darwin visited here in 1835, there were so many land iguanas there was not enough room for him to pitch a tent! I was disappointed to learn that I wouldn't see any here on Santiago. They are prey for the pigs, rats, cats, and dogs brought by the sailing ships. Land iguanas are extinct here and listed as vulnerable on other Galapagos Islands.

The company mining salt tried to start a settlement. It failed and the company released the goats, pigs, donkeys, rats, and mice that had come with the settlers. These invasive species have caused problems. They compete with native animals for food, and they prey on local wildlife. Conservationists are working hard to solve the problem by removing the invasive animals. It is difficult to hunt animals on the rocky ground. So far, all the pigs, goats, and donkeys have been removed from the island. Rats and mice are harder to find and catch.

I noticed tiny *Molluga* plants on my walk. They were growing out of the cracks in the earth made by volcanoes. These plants are a sign that nature is taking hold in new rocky areas. →

Goats were threatening the natural habitat of the giant tortoises in the Galapagos.

Species Introduced to the Galapagos (Since Discovery in 1535)
30 vertebrates (1 fish, 2 frogs, 4 geckos, 10 birds, 13 mammals)
750 plants
543 insecs

21

Field Journal: Day 9

Bartoleme Island

I am heading over to the older islands. Bartoleme Island has two visitor sites. One is at the beach. I am going to snorkel there to see a famous landmark: Pinnacle Rock. It is a tuff cone. Tuff cones are the remains of underwater eruptions. Magma is pushed up from deep beneath Earth's surface. It cools and forms a steep-sided cone that rises out of the water. Pinnacle Rock is a shelter for some species. Galapagos penguins breed in a cave behind the rock. Climate change has threatened the penguins. Warmer ocean currents mean fewer fish, and many penguins starve. Scientists are watching to see if they recover.

Galapagos penguin

Pinnacle Rock

22

After my swim, I headed to the other site. I followed a trail to the highest point on the island. A wooden staircase covers the trail so people won't damage plants or create bare paths where they walk. The Park Service built the wooden structure to also help protect the **fragile** ground from erosion. At the top, I can see the islets known as Daphne Major and Daphne Minor. There are more than 40 islets like these in the Galapagos.

The tequila plant looks dead but isn't. It survives harsh environments with its special leaves. They are covered with gray hairs that hold onto moisture.

natstat STATUS REPORT ST456/part B

Name: Waved albatross
(Phoebastria irrorata)

Threats:
Caught accidentally by line fishers, loss of habitat, climate change making them abandon their nests, illegal egg poaching

Description:

The waved albatross is a very large bird. It has a wingspan of 7–8 feet (2–2.5 meters). It has a cream-colored head and neck, and a bright-yellow bill. These birds waddle when they walk, but they are graceful in the air. They eat squid, fish, and crustaceans. They mate for life and can live for 4–5 years.

Numbers:
25,000–30,000

Status:
Critically endangered

Attach photograph here ➡

23

Field Journal: Day 10

Santa Cruz Island

My next stop is Santa Cruz Island, which is the starting point for most tourists. It has a long history of settlement. There are businesses and homes here. Invasive species have altered the ecosystem. Farming has changed the landscape. In fact, Santa Cruz is the island that has been most affected by human activity. Lava tubes are found on this island, too. They were made by hot lava flowing under the ground. When they cooled, they left tunnels. The tunnels are big enough to walk through. Many tourists visit them each year.

The city of Puerto Ayora lies on the coast of Santa Cruz Island.

24

Santa Cruz is the site of the Charles Darwin Research Station. The visitor center contains exhibits about climate change. It also explains the evolution of plants and animals. It shows how the formation of the islands affected their evolution. Visiting scientists do important research. They study how people can share habitats with wildlife. They are also learning what effects warmer temperatures are having on the health of the ecosystems.

After feral dogs killed off most land iguanas on Santa Cruz, the Darwin Foundation began a breeding program. It settled a new population of iguanas on the nearby islet of Venecia. It even moved enough soil to fill two school buses to create an **artificial** nesting area. The land iguanas are making a comeback in their new home.

Galapagos sea lion injuries are often the result of getting tangled in human-made items. 53 percent of these types of injuries are from fishery items and 47 percent from tourism items.

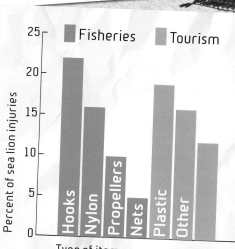

25

Field Journal: Day 11

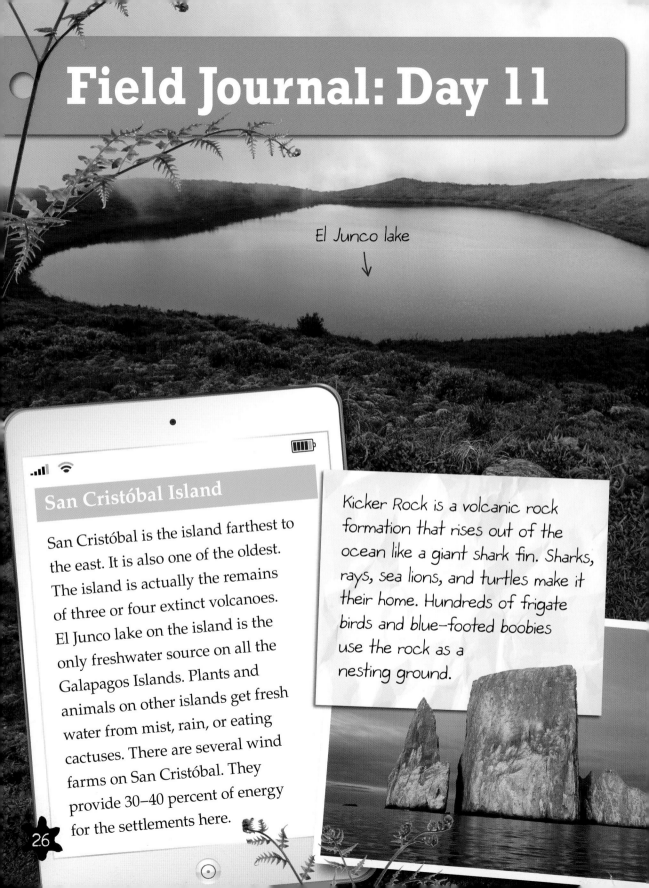

El Junco lake

San Cristóbal Island

San Cristóbal is the island farthest to the east. It is also one of the oldest. The island is actually the remains of three or four extinct volcanoes. El Junco lake on the island is the only freshwater source on all the Galapagos Islands. Plants and animals on other islands get fresh water from mist, rain, or eating cactuses. There are several wind farms on San Cristóbal. They provide 30–40 percent of energy for the settlements here.

Kicker Rock is a volcanic rock formation that rises out of the ocean like a giant shark fin. Sharks, rays, sea lions, and turtles make it their home. Hundreds of frigate birds and blue-footed boobies use the rock as a nesting ground.

26

There are many conservation problems on San Cristóbal. Invasive plants such as the blackberry and guayaba are taking over native plants. Many rare plants are eaten by the feral goats brought by the original settlers. The Galapagos National Park is working to remove the goats. Rangers invited me to join them for a day. With other volunteers, I removed invasive plants and planted native ones.

natstat STATUS REPORT ST456/part B

Name: Galapagos rock purslane
(Calandrinia galapagosa)

Threats:
Habitat destruction, eaten by feral goats

Description:
This is one of the rarest plants on San Cristóbal. At one time, it was found on the northwest side of the island. It no longer exists there. It is a small shrub. It has needle-like leaves that are red or green. The white or pink flowers look like wild roses. It is a favorite plant for feral goats.

Numbers:
Unknown

Status:
Critically endangered

27

Final Report

Cactuses grow in the volcanic landscape of the Galapagos Islands.

REPORT TO:
THE VOLCANIC RESEARCH ORGANIZATION

OBSERVATIONS

Volcanoes formed the Galapagos Islands, and some are still erupting on the younger islands today. This poses a threat to the unique plants and animals that evolved to live in, on, and around the islands. Lava flows create new land on top of existing habitats, destroying plants and animals. Lava flows may cause some rare plants and animals to become extinct. At the same time, they create new habitats for new life to grow. Eruptions are a natural process that cannot be changed, only observed.

28

FUTURE CONCERNS

Other threats to the islands arise from human activities. Early visitors and settlers on the islands brought new plants and animals with them. Invasive plants and animals take space and food sources away from native species. Illegal fishing and the growing number of tourists also cause problems. **Natural resources** such as fresh water are used up. Trails and garbage damage nature. Warmer ocean temperatures change the habitats of fish and sea birds. This affects all life in the islands' food chains.

CONSERVATION PROJECTS

Many people are trying to protect life here. The Darwin Foundation breeds and releases Galapagos tortoises. The National Park Service is building new ranger stations in remote areas. This will help rangers observe and enforce rules to limit fishing and tourism. Conservationists are helping to remove invasive plants and animals. With these projects, it is hoped the unique and rare wildlife on the Galapagos Islands can survive and thrive.

Your Turn

* Pick one of the plants or animals featured in a Status Report in the book. Read the threats to its survival. Make a plan for ways to help conserve it. Will new laws help? Is research needed? Be sure to include ways in which tourists or residents can help.

* Look at the pie chart for the status of animal species in the Galapagos on page 15. Do you think that other ecosystems have similar numbers of critically endangered, endangered, or vulnerable animals? Why or why not? What makes the Galapagos Islands different?

* Write your own journal entry about a time when you watched or interacted with a creature in the wild. What details do you want to include? What made the experience something you remembered?

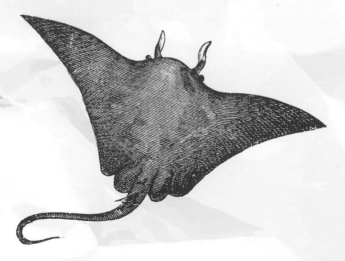

Learning More

BOOKS

Charles Darwin by Laura L. Sullivan (Core Library, 2016)

Galapagos Islands (In Focus) by Clive Gifford (Kingfisher, 2018)

Island: A Story of the Galápagos by Jason Chin (Roaring Brook Press, 2012)

What Is the Theory of Evolution? by Robert Walker (Crabtree Publishing, 2011)

Where Are the Galapagos Islands? by Megan Stine (Grosset & Dunlap, 2017)

WEBSITES

www.natgeokids.com/nz/discover/geography/countries/ng-kids-heads-to-the-galapagos-islands/
Learn all about the Galapagos with National Geographic Kids.

www.scienceforkidsclub.com/galapagos-islands.html
Science for Kids answers all your questions about the Galapagos Islands.

http://video.nationalgeographic.com/video/ecuador_galapagos
National Geographic shows the wonders of the Galapagos in this video.

Glossary & Index

adapt change to suit new surroundings

artificial human-made

bask lie in the sun

biologist a scientist who studies living things

bristles short, stiff hairs

climate change the change in the typical weather conditions in a particular area over a long period of time

conservation preserving or protecting something

craters huge bowl-shaped holes left over from volcanic eruptions

crevice a crack in rock

ecosystem a community of plants and animals all living in the same area

endangered at risk of going extinct

erode when wind or water wears away rocks or other land features

evolution the process by which something develops slowly, from a simple organism to a more complicated one

feral turned wild

fragile easily damaged

invasive species a plant or animal that is not native to an area and spreads easily, damaging the ecosystem

lagoons shallow bays near the shore

lava melted rock that comes out of a volcano

natural resources materials in nature that can be used by people

pavers small flat stones used for pathways

prop roots roots that grow in the air from a trunk down to the ground

prey an animal hunted for food

snorkeling swimming with one's face in the water using a curved tube for breathing

tide the rise and fall of the oceans at different times of day

toxic poisonous

volcanologist someone who studies volcanoes